CONTENTS

PUBLISHED BY COLLET'S (GLASGOW) BOOKSHOP, LTD,
229 HIGH STREET, GLASGOW
PRINTED BY WESTERN PRINTING SERVICES LTD., BRISTOL

THE CLYDE IN WAR TIME

SNAPSHOTS OF A STORMY PERIOD

BY

WILLIAM GALLACHER

INTRODUCTORY

GLASGOW in those epoch-making days of the World War, and the period of revolt which succeeded the Armistice! Never-to-be-forgotten days, the flavour of their struggle and heroism is with us yet, although some of the heroic figures—such as John McLean, Arthur McManus and others—are now no longer living; and other figures, who once played their part in the fight, are now fulfilling anything but heroic roles.

To encompass the happenings of those red-hot days would be impossible in this small volume. I am therefore selecting, from the wealth of material at hand, a few episodes, moving or dramatic, which will give my readers something of the flavour of those days of hard-fought battle. Days when many of us gained valuable experiences for the even harder battles of to-day.

Just prior to the outbreak of war, I was working in the Albion Motor Works. I served as a shop steward, and was also an executive member of the United Brass-founders' Association—later merged with the A.S.E , and then with the A.E.U. I was a member of the British Socialist Party, an ardent propagandist of socialism, and a student of the Marxist teachings expounded by that great revolutionary teacher and

3

fighter, John McLean, the story of whose life is still to be written.

In July 1914, we shop stewards went for our annual summer holidays, determined on our return to make the engineers' shops 100 per cent. solid in preparation for the struggle that lay ahead in November. Notice had been given to the employers that, with the termination of the three years' agreement, a demand would be made for an increase of twopence per hour.

But this was the last carefree holiday for thousands of Clyde workers. Already, when we returned to work, the clouds of war were heavy over Europe. Then, in the first week in August we were swept into the maelstrom.

If wages of engineers had been inadequate before the outbreak of war, they now rapidly became worse. The profiteers were on the job from the first. Prices first, then rents. The housewives' difficulties increased daily.

There was continual agitation in the workshops. Meal-hour discussion circles, with a large sale of revolutionary literature, had for long been common in most Clyde factories; but, following the outbreak of war, these increased vastly in range and importance.

Already, in those early days, we were able to show that every "racketeer," big and little, was on the job. That the war was not in the interests of the workers, but was being used to suppress working-class rights and intensify exploitation. We had considerable support from the workers, but a large number, also, were still under the influence of the Jingo press. However, we continued our agitational and educational work, to rally the workers round our demands in November, when the agreement terminated.

4

THE FEBRUARY STRIKE

By November, the campaign against the war, against high prices and increased rents, and for higher wages, was in full swing. Housewives, as well as factory workers, were being brought into the arena of activity. The Clyde area was beginning to wake up.

As an executive member of my union, I was elected to the Allied Trades Committee, which conducted negotiation with the employers on behalf of the various unions in the engineering trades. The employers made various compromise offers, but would not yield the twopence per hour. Protracted negotiations continued for December and January. In the meantime, the ferment increased on the Clyde, largely contributed to by the splendid work of John McLean.

Then, early in February 1915, while the employers were still adamant in their refusal of the twopence increase, a new "incident" arose, and the whole Clyde area was brought into action.

As a consequence of the rush of war recruits at the outset of war, and the greatly increased demand for output, there was a shortage of skilled workers in the engineering shops. Weirs, of Cathcart, were short of skilled men, so they engaged some in America. These men were to receive a return ticket from the States to Britain, and ten shillings a week higher pay than Weirs' regular employees were getting, and, in addition, a bonus of £10 at the end of six months.

On Feburary 16, following the introduction at Weirs of the higher-paid Americans, the shop stewards called a meeting, and a decision was made for immediate strike

5

action. It was also decided to seek aid from other works, through sympathetic strike action.

On the morning of the 17th there was a consultation of shop stewards at the Albion Motor Works, where I was employed. We decided for action with Weirs, and therefore called a mass meeting for 9 a.m., the breakfast hour. This meeting unanimously supported the proposal for a stoppage. We also got into touch with Yarrow's and Meechan's, to ensure that they also take action. A delegation from Albion proceeded to St. Mungo Hall, where the Weirs strikers were meeting.

When the delegation from the Albion, of which I was leader, arrived at St. Mungo Hall, we found it packed with strikers. The atmosphere was tense.

I was introduced to several shop stewards I had not met before. One of them, J. M. Messer, later became Secretary of the Clyde Workers' Committee. I was then conducted to the platform.

I told the strikers that I brought greetings from the Albion and a pledge of solidarity. I told them Yarrow's and Meechan's were on the move, and that, before the day was over, we would have the whole Clyde closed down. They jumped to their feet—and how they cheered! That morning they had been alone—now all the others were marching into line! Delegates from other factories were now continually arriving at the hall to declare their solidarity. It was as I had predicted: by evening, all the principal factories had decided to close. The great Clyde strike of February 1915 was on!

This strike has been wrongly referred to as an "unofficial strike." This is entirely misleading. Branch and district trade union officials, and in some cases, executive

6

members, like myself, took part. The more correct term would be "spontaneous strike." Such strikes have played an important part in the development of the trade union movement, and are often recognized and supported by the national officials.

We decided to hold mass meetings the following morning in the areas of all the principal factories; and to send a representative from each area to a meeting in the afternoon at which a Central Strike Committee would be formed.

These mass meetings were tremendous, and inspired everyone with a great sense of power. In the afternoon, the representatives met at the "Herald" League bookshop. In order to avoid the penalties of the Defence of the Realm Act, we formed, instead of a Strike Committee, a "Labour-Withholding Committee," with myself as chairman and J. M. Messer as secretary.

The government was exerting every effort to put an end to the strike, endeavouring to influence the national officials of the unions, and succeeding in some cases. All over the country, the press, platform and pulpit was being used to whip up a frenzy of hatred. War fever was spreading; atrocity stories being circulated. Anyone raising his voice in protest was stigmatized as "Pro-German." The press shrieked for action against us, the leaders.

Every morning mass meetings took place in the areas, to which the decisions of the Committee would be reported for approval. The Committee was in session every afternoon and evening. For a fortnight, under the most terrific barrage of opposition ever directed against a strike, we kept going, although not one striker was receiving a penny of strike pay or relief. However, we realized that we could not carry on this way without some disintegration setting in, and this we must avoid at all costs.

We decided, therefore, that the strike would have to be called off. We reported back to the area meetings on these lines, emphasizing the necessity of returning as we had gone out, strong and with organization intact. Every meeting expressed confidence in the committee and pledged support for whatever steps we decided to take.

At the meeting on the night we decided to call off the strike, we had a very serious discussion, and I drew up a resolution, which was adopted, expressing our decision.

This resolution recognized the magnificent response of the workers, and their determination to maintain the fight for the full increase. In the circumstances confronting us, however, it was impossible to continue the strike; and we called on the workers to return as they had come out—as one man.

So far, the resolution was good news to the enemy and his press. But its conclusion sent them into an even more violent paroxysm than had the original strike call. It was as follows: "The strike continues. But now inside the factories. We call on all workers to operate the 'stay-in' strike." Ca'canny was now the order of the day.

It was a great strike. The loyalty and solidarity of the workers could not have been higher. Organization, and co-ordination between factories and areas, and between areas and the centre, was almost perfect. It ended, not on a note of defeat, but with a sense of something achieved. The workers of the Clyde had broken through

8

the atmosphere of war Jingosim and had stood out, strong, unafraid, ready to defend their class against their class enemies.

LLOYD GEORGE COMES TO GLASGOW

Out of the February strike was born a movement destined to endure for some time, and to play a leading part in the struggles of the Clyde. The Strike Committees, formed in each factory of representatives of departments or sections, remained in being as Works Committees, responsible for the organization of the factory. The central body, the "Labour-Withholding Committee," also remained in being.

With the passing of the Munitions Act, made possible by the collaboration of the trade union leaders with Lloyd George, fresh problems arose, of daily occurrence, and the need for some permanent organization became pressing. Out of the "Labour-Withholding Committee," therefore, was formed the Clyde Workers' Committee, of which I was elected chairman, and J. M. Messer, secretary.

During the February strike, the campaign against profiteering in rents began. After the strike, it increased in intensity, becoming a vast and vigorous movement, in which thousands of Glasgow housewives took a militant part. The Clyde Workers' Committee supported the movement, and tremendous demonstrations and parades were held, in which workers from the factories also took part. When the workers commenced to quit the factories to support the demonstrations, the Sheriff of Glasgow communicated by telephone with Lloyd George, minister of munitions. When Lloyd George heard that the men were beginning to leave the factories, he telephoned back, instructing the Sheriff to stop proceedings against workers for the recovery of rent, and promising that "a Rent Restrictions Act will be introduced immediately." Thus, the Glasgow workers and housewives won a victory for all the workers of Britain.

The question of supplying the factories with labour had become an urgent one. Where could additional workers be found? They soon found an answer: employ women. "Dilution of labour" was the official term for this process. We had no objection to "dilution" as long as it was under the control of the working-class organizations, and was not used to lower wages or worsen conditions. But the bosses, of course, sought to use this "patriotic" move as a means to attack trade unionism and conditions.

Lloyd George, minister of munitions, addressed a meeting of employers in Manchester early in December 1915, dealing with this question. In answer to one employer, he said: "You go ahead. If the trade unions interfere, I'll deal with them." I took careful note of this, and filed it away for future reference.

Towards the middle of December, we were informed that Lloyd George would visit Glasgow for two or three days towards Christmas, to get into personal touch with the factories, ending with a conference on "dilution" on Christmas Day. He arrived in Glasgow on Thursday, December 23rd. Previously, upon the advice and persuasion of certain "loyal" trade union officials, he had declared he would have nothing to do with the Clyde Workers' Committee Lloyd George was accompanied by Lord Murray, his deputy, Arthur Henderson, and others.

But, upon his arrival, things began to go badly for the minister. Upon his visit to certain factories, he was told point-blank that the shop stewards would not discuss matters with him unless he first talked with the Clyde Workers' Committee. However, he went ahead with his preparations for the shop stewards' meeting with him on Christmas Day. In the meantime, we of the Workers' Committee had met and decided that the meeting should take place—but that we should be in charge! And, such was the strength of the Workers' Committee movement that it began to be apparent to Lloyd George that he would not be able to hold a shop stewards' conference unless we were called in.

In the meantime, he had had printed a number of tickets for distribution, admitting the bearers to the Christmas Day conference. I have not the space here to go into the details, but by astute manœuvring the Clyde Workers' Committee managed to obtain all these tickets, and were thus able to distribute them—or not to distribute them. This fact, however, did not appear until later when Lloyd George, through Lord Murray had sent for me to take part in a preliminary conference at his hotel.

This was an amusing affair. Lloyd George was absent, so Lord Murray took charge of proceedings. When the fact came out that the Clyde Workers' Committee had secured the tickets, Lord Murray hastened into the next room to consult Lloyd George, who had now returned. He returned with the minister and dismissed everybody.

When they had gone, Lloyd George and Lord Murray came over to me.

"Can you get in touch with the members of your Committee?" Lloyd George asked.

"Yes," I replied.

"Will you arrange for me to meet them this evening?"

"I will," I answered. "We'll meet you here at seven o'clock."

"Thank you, Mr. Gallacher! Thank you!" He was very effusive.

At 6.30 our Committee met to make our final arrangements. At seven, we entered the room where Lloyd George was awaiting us. Lloyd George occupied the central position at the top table, with his colleagues on either side. I was his opposite number at the bottom table, with Johnny Muir, Davey Kirkwood and Arthur McManus on my right; and Messer, Tommy Clarke and some others on my left. We had also added two women workers to the committee.

After some preliminary courtesies on the part of Lloyd George—and some sparring as to procedure, in which we won—Lloyd George got going. He made a typical war propaganda speech, dwelling upon the shortage of men in the factories, and calling on us to support him in this crisis. Yet, only a couple of days earlier, he had stated to the press that he would have nothing to do with us!

I called then upon Johnny Muir, who briefly but ably stated our case. He showed how "dilution" was a feature of capitalism, which had always sought to introduce new

12

types of semi-skilled or unskilled labour at the lowest possible rates. We had no objection to the introduction of new labour, he said. The only question at issue was: who was going to control the process—the workers or the employers? We therefore proposed that the Government take over all factories—out of the employers' hands —and invest the factory committees with full control over matters relating to wages, working conditions and the introduction of new labour.

It was a most able presentation. But, while he was speaking, Lloyd George was doing everything to distract attention from him. It was indeed a pitiful example of uncontrollable egotism. He plucked at his moustache and pawed his hair, looking around to see whether he was the centre of attention

When he began to whisper to Henderson, half turning his back on Johnnie, this was the last straw. I told Johnnie to stop, stating that if Lloyd George did not want to hear us, we would go. After this, the dignitaries at the top table never took their eyes from Johnnie.

After Johnnie, Kirkwood, McManus and the two women spoke. McManus brilliantly stated our position with regard to the war in general, as an imperialist war for trade and territory

Then Lloyd George again took the floor. He fulsomely praised Johnnie Muir's address, but, he said, the proposals were impossible.

"Why not?" I interjected.

"Because," he replied, "it would mean a revolution; and you can't carry through a revolution in the midst of a war."

Only a couple of years later, however, Lenin and the

Bolsheviks showed him just how that very thing *could* be done!

However, on these points, we were too much for him; and he soon brought the discussion to a close. The next item was the meeting on the following day.

Without a smile, Lloyd George proposed the following: Henderson, as chairman, would speak for twenty minutes. Then Lloyd George would speak for fifty minutes, after which he would answer a few written questions. And this was all! This was termed, on the tickets, a "Conference on Dilution!"

We countered with the proposal that Henderson be given two minutes to introduce the speakers. Then half an hour for Lloyd George; and then Johnny Muir to follow with a statement of our views. Then a discussion to take place from the floor.

But this Lloyd George absolutely refused to consider.

"All right!" we said. "You can decide what you and Henderson propose doing, but you can't make the shop stewards listen to you!"

"Oh," said the little man, cockily, "they'll listen to me!"

Upon which the talk broke up.

.   .   .   .   .

Christmas Day, and all eyes were turned towards St. Andrew's Hall where the modern St. George was about to slay the dragon of unrest and conquer the unruly Clyde.

The hall was soon filled with shop stewards. As each one entered, he was amazed by structural changes wrought in the hall. The hall balcony runs right on into the tiers of seats which rise at the back of the platform, so that anyone could move from the balcony onto the tiers and down to the platform.

But not so, on this Christmas Day! On each end of the balcony, near the platform tiers, which were unoccupied, powerful barricades had been erected. Lined across the hall in front of the platform were several rows of police. St. George was well protected.

Our boys now began to sing, and kept it up until the platform party came on Then they all rose and gave them the "Red Flag." The platform stood until they had concluded.

Henderson then stood up to speak, and the storm broke. After vain attempts to be heard, he made a gesture and Lloyd George arose. He pranced up and down the platform. He waved his hands, stretching them out in mute appeal.

During a comparative lull, he shouted, "I appeal to you in the name of our late friend, Keir Hardie!"

At the mention of Hardie's name, the "Red Flag" again resounded. Lloyd George stormed and threatened, screamed and shouted, the sweat pouring down his face, but all to no purpose. When he stopped, through sheer exhaustion, a signal was given and Johnnie Muir mounted a seat. There was instant silence, and Johnnie began to speak

Lloyd George, Henderson and the others walked off the platform, leaving the meeting in our hands. Immediately after the meeting, a lying "official" report was issued which the press printed. The Glasgow *Forward* published a true report and was at once suppressed.

ARREST AND PRISON LIFE

WE of the Clyde Workers' Committee had for some time felt the need of a paper of our own. We managed to get together the scanty capital, and by the middle of January 1916, *The Worker* appeared, with Johnnie Muir as editor.

Surely there never was a paper so eagerly received! Those of us who wrote for the paper put our hearts into it. By the time the fifth issue was on the press the blow fell. In issue Number Four an article had appeared, written by an I.L.P. pacifist, entitled, "Should the Workers Arm?" This was used as the pretext for persecuting us.

Johnnie Muir and I were arrested, as was also Walter Bell, manager of the S.L.P. Press who printed our paper. It was late on a cold winter night when we were thrown into the cells in the Northern Police Station.

John Wheatley had engaged the solicitor, Rosslyn Mitchell, to take charge of our case. In the morning we came before a magistrate and were consigned to the Sheriff who committed us to prison pending our trial in the High Court.

We were charged with "having on or about January 29th at 50, Renfrew Street or elsewhere in Glasgow, attempted to cause mutiny, sedition or disaffection among the civilian population and to impede, delay and restrict the production of war material by producing, printing, publishing and circulating among workers in and around Glasgow engaged on war materials, a newspaper entitled *The Worker*."

The following morning, we were let out on bail of £50 each.

While out on bail, I made a journey with Johnnie Muir to London to see the ministry of munitions with regard to the question of "dilution" Strikes had broken out on the Clyde, owing to this question, resulting in the arrest of Kirkwood, Messer, McManus, Bridges, Wainwright, Tommy Clarke, and others, who were all deported from Glasgow. It was Wheatley who proposed that Johnnie and I go to London to get the ministry to agree to make the same rule apply to all factories as it did to the factories where Johnnie and I worked—namely, full freedom of inspection. We were also to get the ministry to obtain withdrawal of the deportation order.

We wasted our time in London, conversations eventually leading to nothing, although Pringle did his best, obtaining an interview with Dr. Addison for us, and defending our hopes in the House of Commons. We returned after only two days, but could see the situation was hopeless for the time being. Parkhead was out, but with only Dalmuir, Albion and Meechans supporting them. When, a few days after, Parkhead went back, the strike movement collapsed.

. . . . .

In the meantime, however, the general agitation against war had been growing in intensity. In this McLean played a very important part. Every day he was at the factory gates, from one end to the other of the Clyde. Every night he spoke on the streets, in halls or lecture rooms. He was developing scores of new agitators. We should have realized that the Government would soon take action, but while we had McLean's dynamic personality in agitation, and a strong workshop organization through our factory committees and the Central Clyde Workers' Committee, there was no experienced political leadership to weld these forces together.

When the attack came, therefore, we could not meet it. On Sunday, February 6, McLean was arrested by the military authorities and confined in Edinburgh Castle. But they soon handed him over to the civil authorities who committed him for trial and released him on bail. Then, James Maxton, McDougall, and Jack Smith—an English anarchist—were arrested on charges of sedition.

Thus, a considerable number of us were awaiting trial. Edinburgh High Court was fixed as the venue for our trials. And a zeppelin raid had just taken place over that city! Add to this, that we were accused in the press of being German agents.

Eventually, McLean came up for trial, and it was a memorable, fighting trial, an example which I wish we others had followed McLean defied his enemies—his speech from the dock was a masterpiece. He was sentenced to three years' penal servitude.

The next trial was that of Johnnie Muir, Walter Bell and myself. We appeared in the same court as McLean —but what a contrast! Even now it is hard to think of it without a feeling of shame.

Our counsel tried to persuade me to keep out of the witness-box, arguing that the prosecution might force from me the authorship of the article. But I insisted on taking the stand. They asked me, had I written the article in the *Worker*? No. Who had written it? I did not know. Did I approve of the editor publishing it? Yes.

Had I refrained from going into the witness-box, it

18

would not have affected our fate. Our conviction was assured, from the beginning. It was a rotten business all through, and my only satisfaction was that, by going into the box, I was able to share responsibility with Johnnie Muir. A bold stand in court would have aroused wider protest among the workers on our behalf. The heroic conduct of Dimitrov at the Leipzig trial has shown all workers the value of a courageous stand under such circumstances, however perilous.

A verdict of "Guilty" was brought in, and the following day, Muir and I were sentenced to twelve months' imprisonment. Walter Bell received three months A week later, Maxton and McDougall also received twelve months, and Jack Smith eighteen months.

We were all sent to Calton Gaol, McLean, however, only for a fortnight, afterwards being transferred to Peterhead Convict Prison. Calton Gaol, which has now been pulled down, was built in 1816. It was by far the worst prison in Scotland; cold, silent and repellent. Its discipline was extremely harsh, and the diet atrocious. There was no "association" labour. Most of the prisoners worked in their cells at mat-making and similar occupations.

The one hour's exercise in the morning was the sole opportunity we had of seeing each other, when desperate attempts were made to exchange a whisper or two. For breakfast, we had thick porridge and sour milk For dinner, soup and a piece of dry bread. And for supper, thick porridge and sour milk.

Unfortunately, poor health, prison confinement—but, mainly, the whispered suggestions of a semi-crazed member of our movement, which had preyed on his

19

mind—had seriously affected McDougall, so that he began to have illusions of persecution.

One Sunday morning, after we had been in about six weeks, we were seated in chapel awaiting the chaplain's entrance. As he came in and approached the pulpit, McDougall stood up and shouted, "Sir, I want you to write to my father. The warders are talking at my door at night, trying to drive me insane."

Two warders led him back to his cell. Later that day, he had a terrible nervous attack. It was a heart-breaking experience to have to sit in one's cell and listen to him, without being able to do anything to help. Of course, no one had been talking at his door at night. The warders all went home after the prisoners had gone to bed, except for the officer at the gate-house. And only a watchman in rubber-soled sneakers made the rounds at night. It was not possible to talk in any part of the hall without the sound being heard in every cell.

To illustrate this, Maxton occupied the next cell to mine. At "Nine o'clock bell" —bed-time—I made it a practice to tap the verse of the "Red Flag" on the wall, while Maxton contributed the chorus, after which I gave an alleged rendering of "Hip, Hip, Hurrah!" After a month of these daily tapping obbligatos, a prisoner on an upper tier complained about the noise, and Maxton was removed to another cell.

The day after his breakdown, McDougall was transferred to Perth for special care. Following this affair, questions were asked in the Commons regarding conditions in Calton Gaol. It was decided, therefore, that certain officials, together with a representative of organized labour, should pay a visit to the prison.

We knew nothing of all this, so I was quite surprised, one day, when eating dinner in my cell, when my door opened and an imposing deputation entered. The Chief Warder explained that these were some gentlemen from the Home Office who had come to see how I was getting on. How did I like my work, someone questioned. There was a small engineer shop in the gaol, with a very capable engineer warder in charge. He was responsible for all repair work in the prison. I worked under him, and spent my time going around from one part of the prison to another. I talked to warders and to prisoners. Periodically I managed to visit the place where Maxton was working, and had a chat with him. Sometimes, I was able to get a few words with Johnnie Muir. So, when asked about my job, I said it was "all right." I said I had had worse jobs and, if only I could get out at night, I could stick it long enough.

Later, I heard that David Low, a Labour man, was in that commission, supposedly looking for faults in the prison system. Had any of us been asked about these, we could have given plenty of examples

On Saturday, February 3, 1917, Maxton and McDougall were released. On February 13, Muir and I came out.

When I returned to the same prison two and a half years later, a group of warders, headed by the Chief Warder, met me at the door of the "Reception." The Chief stepped forward and held out his hand as he said: "Well, it's an old friend back again." And all the others followed suit.

THE GREAT STRIKE OF JANUARY 1919

RELEASED from prison, I again flung myself into activities. Space is too limited in this short booklet to detail the great revival of revolutionary activitity on the Clyde, later on; the campaign for John McLean's release; the tremendous inspiration, which gave new life to the Clyde movement, of the triumph of the Russian workers, led by the Bolshevik Party, over their oppressors and exploiters. The re-establishment of the Clyde Workers' Committee; the futile visit of Aucland Geddes to Glasgow; John McLean's release after serving only seven months of a five years' sentence; the end of the war and the ex-soldiers' return; the return of the famous "deportees" to Glasgow—all this is material for a book, a book which, amidst the exigencies of the struggle, I am trying to write.

But, for the present selection of Clyde snapshots, I must pick January 1919, when I returned from a short holiday at Rothesay with a busy time ahead of me. Our factory movement had gained terrific strength and momentum, and we were full of courage and enterprise. Strike action for a shorter working-week was our object.

We knew that a strike call would secure the response of all the principal factories of the Clyde. At our great shop stewards' conference, on January 18, 1919, at which 500 delegates were present, a deputation, representing the Glasgow Trades Council and the trade union officials, appeared, asking to participate in the strike call and the direction of the strike. We gave them a welcome, and then settled down to prepare the call and to appoint a responsible leading committee.

We appointed an equal number of officials and shop

stewards on the committee with two joint secretaries: Wm Shaw, secretary of the Trades Council, and Dave Morton, a shop steward. Emmanuel Shinwell was made chairman, while I was made organizer of the strike. Our strike call ran as follows:

"The Joint Committee representing the official and unofficial sections of the industrial movement, having considered the reports of the shop stewards and representatives in the various industries, hereby resolve to demand a forty-hour working week for all workers, as an experiment with the object of absorbing the unemployed. If a forty-hour week fails to give the desired result, a more drastic reduction of hours will be demanded. A general strike has been declared to take place on Monday, January 24, and all workers are expected to respond.
"By Order of the Joint Committee, Representing
All Workers."

When the day arrived, the stoppage was practically complete. The principal factories struck to a man. It was a great strike—but it did not have great leadership. We were strike leaders, and no more. We were all agreed as to the importance of the strike for the forty-hour week, but we had never discussed a general strike against capitalism. Rather less complacency, and more political understanding would have been an advantage, also. Thousands of workers were following our lead, but our leadership had no real plan or unity of purpose—already rifts showed between official and unofficial leadership. Throughout the country, reactionary national union officials were seeking to discredit or undermine us. And we lacked the necessary unity and political knowledge to counteract this.

However, the solidarity and fighting spirit of the workers was magnificent. On the Wednesday morning we had a march and demonstration to George's Square, where a deputation, led by Shinwell, went into the City Chambers. I was not clear as to the purpose of this move, and was surprised. It appeared that the deputation had informed the Lord Provost of our demand for a forty-hour week. The Lord Provost had promised to wire our demand to the government, and to let us have a reply on the Friday, if one were forthcoming. We therefore dispersed, after reporting to the crowd, with the intention of again mustering in the Square on Friday.

On the morning of Friday, January 31, the Clyde district was early astir. From all parts, workers came streaming into George's Square. With one or two comrades beside me, I addressed the huge gathering from the plinth of the Gladstone statue while the deputation, headed by Shinwell, and strengthened by Neil McLean, M.P., went in to see the Lord Provost.

The footpath and roadway in front of the monument were packed with strikers. Towards the post office, at the south-east corner, there was a terrific jam. Lined up against the Municipal Buildings, and in the rear of the strikers, were several rows of police.

Suddenly, and without any warning, the police made a savage assault on the rear of the meeting, smashing right and left with their batons, utterly regardless of whom they struck. The fact that women and children were in the crowd mattered nothing to these "guardians of the peace." Their onslaught on defenceless workers was made with brutal ferocity.

There was a sudden and irresistible surge forward of

24

the strikers, and, before any of us on the plinth could realize what had happened, the whole mass was rushing towards the west side of the Square, the police still attacking them from behind

Rain had fallen during the night, and the ground was wet and muddy. Just below where I stood, a woman was lying on her side. On her face were the marks of a muddy boot. This I saw with my own eyes. We jumped off the plinth and, as the others stopped to raise the injured woman, I ran across the Square to where the Chief Constable stood, with a guard of some ten policemen about him, supervizing the proceedings.

The only thing that saved me then was that too many of them tried to club me at once and they got in each other's way. Before I was battered to the ground, I managed to get in a "full-power" upper cut which caught a constable on the chin and nearly lifted his head off. I fell on my back, and began to try and raise myself. I saw the policeman whom I had hit, standing over me with his baton raised. He was about to smash my face in, and I was too weak to defend myself. Suddenly someone plunged down on top of me, and the baton landed, not on me, but on the comrade who had dived in to save me. He was Neil Alexander—I didn't know him, but had seen him before—a boilermaker, a quiet, unassuming but splendid comrade. I got to know him well later on.

We were dragged to our feet. Blood rushed from my head, streaming over my face and neck, and I was plastered with mud. We were then half-dragged across the Square towards the Municipal Buildings.

By now a change had taken place in the Square. The strikers were now facing the police and fighting back.

They had them at a standstill. The noise was deafening and penetrated easily to the quiet of the council corridor, where, all this time, the deputation had been patiently waiting to see the Lord Provost, who had no intention of receiving them.

One of the deputation looked out of the window and discovered that a battle was raging. This brought them all out with a rush, Davie Kirkwood leading. He got out to the middle of the roadway just as I was being dragged towards the Council doorway. He had just raised his arms in a gesture of protest when a police-sergeant, approaching him from the rear, brought down his baton with terrific force on the back of his head. I have never seen a more cowardly or unjustified blow.

Neil McLean saw the vicious blow and rushed forward, protesting vigorously. They were probably rather scared because he was a Member of Parliament, or he would have got the same treatment.

Kirkwood was picked up unconscious and, together with Neil Alexander and myself, was carried to the quadrangle of the Municipal Buildings. Someone gave me a piece of white linen which I bound round my head, to stop the bleeding.

Enraged by the brutal and wanton attack upon them, and still further infuriated by news of the smashing which Kirkwood and I had received, the workers rushed bare-handed at the police and drove them right across the Square. The Sheriff emerged from the City Chambers with the Lord Provost and read the Riot Act.

When, later, we were on trial for rioting and inciting to riot, the police witnesses, one after the other, swore that the trouble started with stone-throwing by the strikers.

They swore that the air was black with stones, chunks of iron, bottles. Yet, at the time when they swore the stone-throwing started, the police were standing in front of the Chambers.

Well, the whole front of the Chambers is one long row of windows, while, in front of the doorway, stand four lamp-posts, each with a cluster of seven arc-lamp globes. Yet not a window or lamp was broken. Press photographs, taken a little later, also revealed this, and likewise did not show a single missile lying on the ground!

The fighting was still proceeding in the Square. The strikers had constructed impromptu barricades out of boxes of mineral-water bottles, taken from a lorry. Attempts of the police to rush the barricades were unsuccessful.

Inside, we had been removed from the quadrangle into one of the corridors. We did not know how the fight was going, except that, in the earlier stages, workers were being brought in to receive first-aid; and, later, it was policemen who were being carried in for a similar purpose. We then knew that things were going a different way. Then the battle appeared to be coming nearer the Chambers. We were removed from the corridor to a room upstairs where we were shut in with several policemen

In a few minutes our comrade, "Jock" McBain, came in, with his head in a bandage. He said the police had been driven right up against the Chambers. The leaders wanted the crowd now to march to Glasgow Green for a great protest demonstration. But they would not leave without word from us. Would we speak to them from the balcony? This we eventually did, after some discussion, and the strikers formed up and marched off to the Green.

We were, of course, kept under arrest. That night they also arrested Shinwell, and, during the next few days, Harry Hopkins, George Ebury, Young Brennan and several others. We were all kept in Duke Street Prison. On the Saturday, troops marched in and took possession of the city.

A week later, the strike was called off, and the Clyde settled down to normal life once more. Then, two weeks later, we were all let out on bail, pending trial.

The closing episode of the "revolt" took place the following April, in the High Court, Edinburgh, when Shinwell, Kirkwood, Hopkins, Ebury, Brennan, Alexander and myself came up for trial. I had decided to forgo counsel and defend myself, in which decision the Clyde Workers' Committee supported me. Walter C. Leechman, a solicitor, and old member of the Labour Party, gave us legal advice, and we greatly appreciated his services.

The trial opened with a great array of witnesses for the prosecution—mostly policemen, but with the Sheriff of Lanarkshire and the Lord Provost of Glasgow thrown in. We managed somewhat to shake the evidence of these witnesses before the jury. When the prosecution's case was concluded, I suggested we submit our case without calling witnesses for the defence, as they had no case against us. I was overborne, however. One of our witnesses, however, almost sunk the ship for us. He entered the box with a real "tough" look on his face. When the judge began to repeat to him the words of the oath, he said:

"Awa' wi' yi'—yer sittin' up there like a Punch and Judy in the Circus!" "Take that man away!" roared the judge.

After counsel had addressed the jury on behalf of the others, I also spoke. I dealt with the strike and the demonstrations arising from it. Then, I went on to the police attack, describing the scene as I had observed it from the plinth. How I had jumped down to expostulate with the Chief Constable, and how the police had rushed at me.

"I am accused of having struck certain policemen," I said. "This part of the evidence is true. I struck out—I struck hard. My only regret is that I did not have greater strength, to strike harder."

I concluded by declaring my determination to keep up the fight.

"Gentlemen," I stated, "it is for you to decide. You can decide whether I'll sleep to-night in my own home or in a prison cell; but, believe me, whichever it is, I'll sleep with an easy conscience."

Without loss of time, the jury returned a verdict of "Not Guilty" on all the prisoners except Shinwell and myself. Shinwell was sentenced to five months' imprisonment, and I to three.

Thus ended the great January Strike of the Clyde workers.

CONCLUSION

ON Sunday, February 23, 1919, I was released on bail, after the great battle in the Square, during the January Strike, which I have just described.

On Monday, February 24, Philip Snowden was speaking in the Town Hall, in my home town, Paisley. Before the meeting I went behind the platform for a chat with him. He shook hands warmly and said: "You did well —very well. But you'll have to do better next time."

Yes, there will be a "next time." But with a leadership worthy of the courage and heroism of the workers. The one lesson which stands out, from all that happened on the Clyde in those days—both from our successes as well as our failures—is that the might of the working class is invincible, if only the leadership is there, adequate to the tasks confronting it

How may such a leadership be developed? I found my answer to this question in 1920, when I attended the Second World Congress of the Communist International, to which I had been invited as a representative of the Clyde shop stewards.

As I had no passport then, I had to travel as a stowaway, from Newcastle, on a ship bound for Bergen, in Norway. This I did with the help of one of the firemen who was a comrade. From Bergen, the local Communists aided me to sail as passenger to Vardo, and from there I travelled in a little motor fishing-boat to Nurminsk, in Russia. And from thence to the Congress in Moscow.

At this Congress I engaged in discussions which eventually completely altered my views on revolutionary politics.

But it was not easy—this change. The shop steward movement was still comparatively strong then, and I had very little regard for political parties or for parliamentary action. I was an oustanding example of the "Left sectarian," and Lenin referred to me as such in his book on *Left-Wing Communism: an Infantile Disorder*.

But here I was in company of Lenin himself, and other international figures, arguing, discussing these views. I was hard to convince but, as the discussions proceeded, I began to realize the weakness of my position. More and more, the clear, simple arguments of Lenin were impressed on my mind. I had never had such an experience before, as when I talked with Lenin. Here was a man upon whom the eyes of the world were turned, who was making history—yet simple, unaffected, a true comrade in the deepest sense of the word. The remarkable thing about him was his complete subordination of self. His whole mind and being were centred on the revolution.

And the more I talked with Lenin and others, the more I came to see what the Party of the workers meant, in the revolutionary struggle. A Party of revolutionary workers, winning over the trade unions and co-operatives by the correctness of its policy. A Party with no interests but in the working class, and the agricultural and small middle-class allies of the working class. Such a Party—using every means of expression—could make an exceptionally valuable platform of Parliament for energetic struggle on behalf of the workers, and against the capitalist enemy. With a powerful Party of this nature, the whole strength of the working class and its allies can be brought into action. Such a Party is absolutely essential to lead the advance of the working class.

—

CPSIA information can be obtained
at www.ICGtesting.com
Printed in the USA
BVHW041057230119
538451BV00018B/1039/P